11/20

ANTS

KENNY ABDO

Fly!
An Imprint of Abdo Zoom
abdobooks.com

abdobooks.com

Published by Abdo Zoom, a division of ABDO, P.O. Box 398166, Minneapolis, Minnesota 55439. Copyright © 2020 by Abdo Consulting Group, Inc. International copyrights reserved in all countries. No part of this book may be reproduced in any form without written permission from the publisher. Fly!™ is a trademark and logo of Abdo Zoom.

Printed in the United States of America, North Mankato, Minnesota.
102019
012020

THIS BOOK CONTAINS RECYCLED MATERIALS

Photo Credits: Everette Collection, iStock, Shutterstock, ©Copeinator123 Tales to Astonish Vol 1 35 p9 / CC-BY-SA
Production Contributors: Kenny Abdo, Jennie Forsberg, Grace Hansen
Design Contributors: Dorothy Toth, Neil Klinepier

Library of Congress Control Number: 2019941318

Publisher's Cataloging-in-Publication Data

Names: Abdo, Kenny, author.
Title: Ants / by Kenny Abdo
Description: Minneapolis, Minnesota : Abdo Zoom, 2020 | Series: Superhero animals |
    Includes online resources and index.
Identifiers: ISBN 9781532129476 (lib. bdg.) | ISBN 9781098220457 (ebook) |
    ISBN 9781098220945 (Read-to-Me ebook)
Subjects: LCSH: Ants--Juvenile literature. | Ants--Behavior--Juvenile literature. |
    Insect behavior--Juvenile literature. | Entomology--Juvenile literature. |
    Zoology--Juvenile literature.
Classification: DDC 595.796--dc23

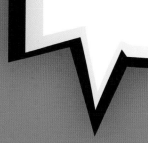

TABLE OF CONTENTS

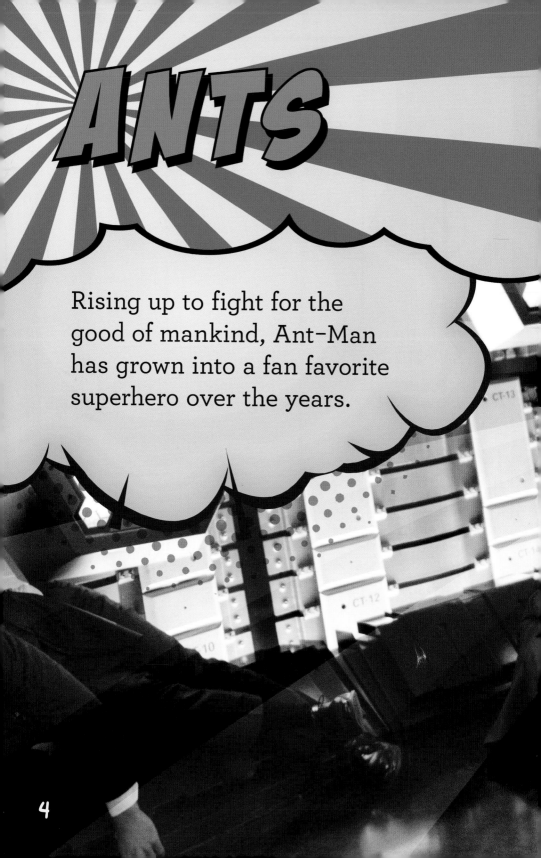

ANTS

Rising up to fight for the good of mankind, Ant-Man has grown into a fan favorite superhero over the years.

5

With more than 12,000 **species**, ants can be found all around the world. From your picnic basket to the jungles of the Amazon, you'll find them just about everywhere. The only place they don't live is Antarctica.

ORIGIN STORY

Ant-Man first appeared in *Tales to Astonish* issue 35 in 1962. Stan Lee, along with his partners Jack Kirby and Larry Lieber, created the pint-sized hero.

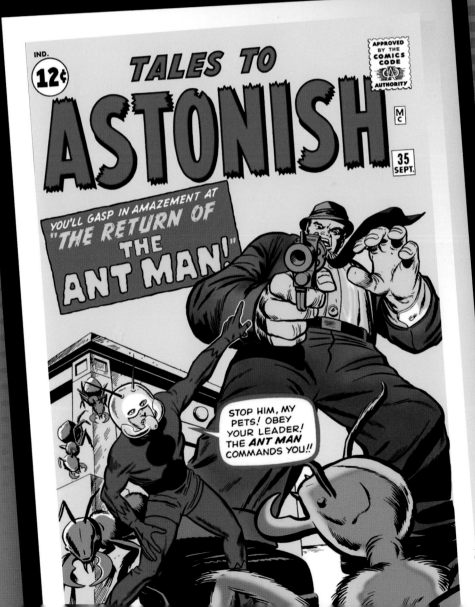

Scientist Hank Pym first donned the red and black suit. He invented a gas that could alter the size of humans. Career thief Scott Lang unwittingly stole the suit, becoming the hero he was meant to be.

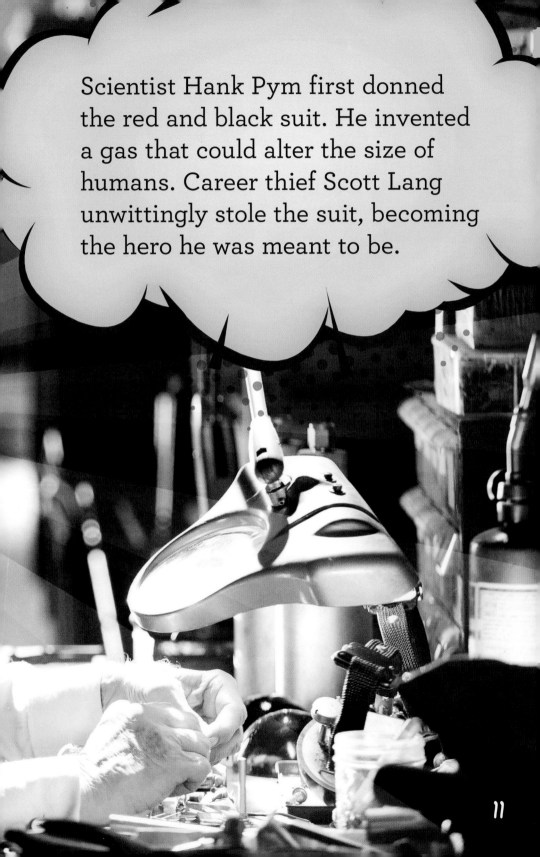

POWERS & ABILITIES

A single ant can carry up to 5,000 times its own weight!

13

Ants work together to both build and carry things. They are one of the few insects to **embrace** teamwork.

mandible

Ants hold the record for the fastest movement in the insect world. The trap-jaw ant can close its mandible at 140 mph (225.3 kph). This is used to trap prey or fight other ants.

Ants "hear" by feeling vibrations through their feet. Ants use their **antennae** to communicate with each other.

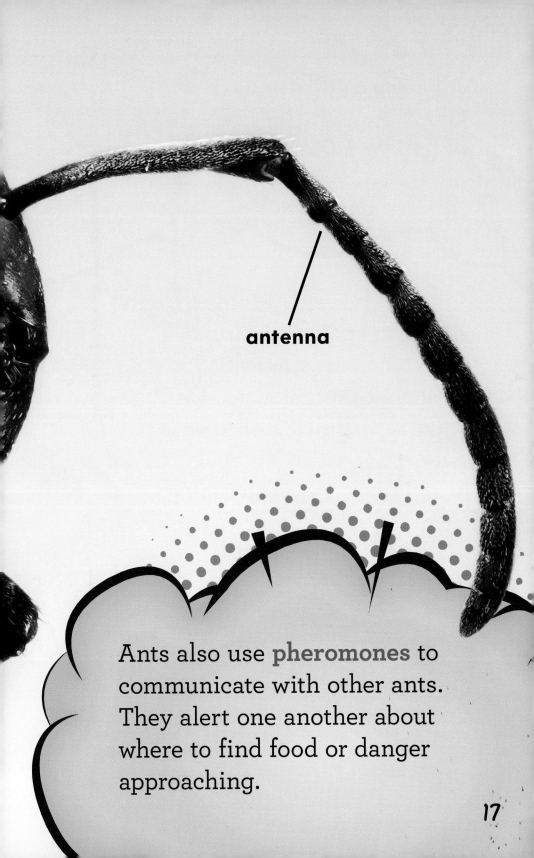

antenna

Ants also use **pheromones** to communicate with other ants. They alert one another about where to find food or danger approaching.

IN ACTION

Like the insect, Ant-Man packs big power in small form. The Ant-Man suit allows Scott Lang to shrink several sizes. He retains his full-sized strength even when he's tiny.

The Ant-Man helmet allows Lang to talk with and direct the actions of ants and other insects. Kind of like high-tech **pheromones**!

Scott Lang was a master thief before becoming a hero. Like ants, he can slip in and out of anywhere he wants without being detected. The Ant-Man suit just allows him to look good while doing it!

GLOSSARY

antenna – one of the two long, thin body parts that sticks out from an insect's head that is used to feel, smell, and communicate.

embrace – to take up or accept easily.

mandible – one of the front biting mouth parts on insects.

pheromone – a chemical substance animals release to signal others within their species. Pheromones help animals establish territories, attract mates, and warn of danger.

prey – an animal hunted or killed by another animal for food.

species – living things that are very much alike.

ONLINE RESOURCES

Booklinks
NONFICTION NETWORK
FREE! ONLINE NONFICTION RESOURCES

To learn more about ants, please visit abdobooklinks.com or scan this QR code. These links are routinely monitored and updated to provide the most current information available.

INDEX